D1243129

Machines at Work

Airplanes

by Rebecca Stromstad Glaser

Bullfrog
Books

Ideas for Parents and Teachers

Bullfrog Books give children practice reading nonfiction at the earliest levels. Repetition, familiar words, and photos support early readers.

Before Reading

- Discuss the cover photo with the class. What does it tell them?
- Look at the picture glossary together. Read and discuss the words.

Read the Book

- "Walk" through the book and look at the photos. Let the child ask questions.
- Read the book to the child, or have him or her read independently.

After Reading

- Prompt the child to think more. Ask: What types of airplanes have you seen? Where did you see them?

Bullfrog Books are published by Jump!
5357 Penn Avenue South
Minneapolis, MN 55419
www.jumplibrary.com

Library of Congress Cataloging-in-Publication Data
Glaser, Rebecca Stromstad.
 Airplanes / by Rebecca Stromstad Glaser.
   p. cm. — (Bullfrog books. Machines at work)
 Audience: K to grade 3
 Summary: "This photo-illustrated book for early readers describes different types of airplanes and the jobs they do. Includes photo glossary" —Provided by publisher.
 Includes bibliographical references and index.
 ISBN 978-1-62031-021-2 (hardcover)
 1. Airplanes—Juvenile literature. I. Title.
 TL547.G53 2013
 629.133'34—dc23

                                        2012008571

Series Editor: Rebecca Glaser
Series Designer: Ellen Huber
Photo Researcher: Heather Dreisbach

Photo Credits: Dreamstime, 7, 17, 20-21, 23f; Getty Images, 1, 4, 5, 12, 13, 23e; iStockphoto, 6; Newscom, 18, 23d; Shutterstock, 3a, 10, 16, 19, 22, 23b, 24; Superstock, 8-9; U.S. Air Force, 11, 14, 15, 23a, 23c

Printed in the United States of America at Corporate Graphics, North Mankato, Minnesota.
7-2012 / 1122
10 9 8 7 6 5 4 3 2 1

Table of Contents

Airplanes at Work

Pilots fly airplanes.

What planes
do they fly?

Look in the sky.

Jet planes fly high.
They carry lots of people.

They go
to cities
far away.

Crop planes fly low.

sprayer

They spray crops.
Then bugs stay away.

Cargo planes fly far.
They take mail.
They take food.

A big cargo plane even holds a tank.

tank

Spy planes fly very high.

Spies take pictures.
They watch the enemy.

Fighter planes
fly in war.

They are fast!

They shoot at
the enemy.

15

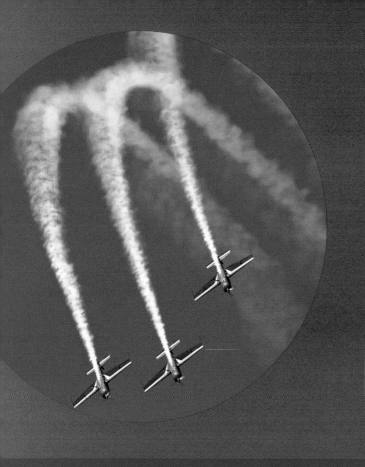

Stunt planes fly in air shows.

They fly in a circle.

They fly upside down.

ski

Ski planes land on
snow or ice.

They do not need
a runway.

19

Where do you see planes?

Parts of a Plane

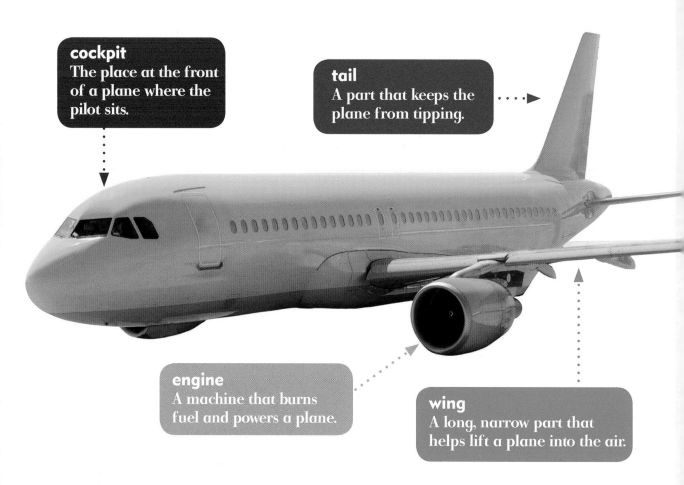

cockpit
The place at the front of a plane where the pilot sits.

tail
A part that keeps the plane from tipping.

engine
A machine that burns fuel and powers a plane.

wing
A long, narrow part that helps lift a plane into the air.

Picture Glossary

cargo plane
A large plane made to carry goods.

ski plane
A plane with skis for landing and taking off on snow and ice.

crop plane
A small plane that flies low and sprays plants.

spy plane
A plane that flies very high and takes pictures of the enemy.

fighter plane
A fast plane made to turn quickly and shoot the enemy.

stunt plane
A small plane flown in air shows to do tricks.

Index

To Learn More

Learning more is as easy as 1, 2, 3.

1) Go to www.factsurfer.com

2) Enter "airplane" into the search box.

3) Click the "Surf" button to see a list of websites.

With factsurfer.com, finding more information is just a click away.